Third Eye Awakening

The complete guide to opening your third eye, and developing your psychic abilities!

Table of Contents

Introduction

Thank you for taking the time to pick up this book on awakening your third eye.

This book covers the topic of third eye awakening and will teach you to unlock and develop your psychic abilities. Everyone has psychic abilities lying dormant within them, but sadly, very few people ever access these abilities.

In order to access these psychic powers such as intuition, clairvoyance, and the ability to view auras, it's essential that you first awaken your third eye. Once your third eye has been awakened and you become truly in tune with your body, these hidden skills and abilities will begin to develop.

In the follow chapters we will discuss how exactly you can awaken your third eye through a range of strategies, such as chakra balancing and specific meditation exercises.

Once again, thanks for choosing this book, I hope you find it to be helpful!

Chapter 1: What is the Third Eye?

The third eye, also referred to as the Pineal eye, is the point on your brow in the middle of your eyes where the Pineal gland is located. It is said to be the focal point of your sixth sense, and where occult power originates from. Tapping in to your third eye is essential if you'd like to access and develop your psychic abilities.

While you probably know some people who can access their third eye effortlessly, most people struggle in this endeavor. This struggle has resulted in a large number of people denying the existence of a third eye altogether.

What most people do not realize is that all of us have a third eye and we can all access it – and further enhance it – through proper and intensive meditation. It can make us capable of achieving our maximum level of knowledge, as it allows us to perceive the past, present, and future.

Also referred to as the inner eye or the mind's eye, this concept is referred to as an energy that can be used to tap into what we can't see, taste, feel, hear, or smell. In other words, whatever can't be felt by our five senses can be conveniently accessed by our third eye.

Our sixth sense is also referred to as the spiritual chakra. It can expose us to great wisdom, but only if we allow it to guide us. If you develop your ability to use your third eye, you will be able to see the unseen. You will be able to develop such skills as clairvoyance, telepathy, lucid dreaming, augmented imagination, and visualization.

Even in the womb, we were able to use our five senses. We could already hear voices and noises. We could feel it when somebody would touch the stomach of our pregnant mother. We could thumb suck and taste however our thumb tasted while inside our mother's tummy – and smell however our thumb smelled too. We could not see very well at that time, but we could see light. We should be grateful that we can experience life to the fullest because of these five incredible senses. However, can we really use the term "fullest" to describe how we live our lives knowing that there is this sixth sense that can ultimately give us an experience that our five senses cannot?

Have you ever experienced thinking about something and then, surprisingly, it happened in reality? We commonly describe this as a coincidence, don't we?

You have also probably experienced feeling as if someone seemed to be watching you, and so you looked up, only to find out that, yes, someone was indeed watching you!

You may refer to these scenarios as coincidences, but those were experiences in which your third eye was trying to lead you. And if you strongly believe in the existence of your sixth sense, these "coincidences" should serve as your proof that you can indeed hone your skills in using your third eye.

Developing and opening your third eye will allow you to have a better life in general. It can ultimately address personal, professional, emotional, mental, and spiritual issues. If you have problems in terms of your career or finances, you can use your third eye to become enlightened on how to address such problems. The same thing goes when you have relationship problems whether with your partner, family, relatives, friends, and colleagues.

This book will teach you how to awaken you third eye, develop the different psychic abilities, and put such skills to good use to make your life – and the lives of others – better.

Chapter 2: Awakening the Third Eye

In this chapter, we will discuss several steps that can help you awaken your third eye.

HOW CAN YOU AWAKEN YOUR THIRD EYE?

1. Bolster peace and calmness.

    Bolster the peace and calmness of your mind. It doesn't necessarily have to be through meditation. It can be by focusing on a specific activity that you love doing such as watching TV or reading a book. The important thing is that it can effectively make your feel relaxed and calm.

    If and when you are using your third eye, you have to be attentive lest you fail to listen to the message that it wants to convey. This is the reason behind the importance of bolstering peace and calmness. It can be difficult to hear the message if there is noise around you.

2. Develop your intuition.

    There are several strategies to hone your intuition. One of which is exerting effort in learning about dream interpretation. There are many books on this topic that will help you find the meaning of your dreams and figure out how you can relate it to reality.

    Another way is learning the skill of lucid dreaming, in which case, you are aware that you are dreaming, and you are in control of whatever you're dreaming about.

    If and when you decide to explore these strategies, make sure that you are having fun doing it. Maintain the calmness of your mind to ensure that you achieve the desired results. However, don't expect to succeed on your first few tries. You have to be patient in developing these skills.

3. Bolster your creativity.

   Hone your creative skills by doing something you have not done before, something that will bring out the best in you, and something that will make you stretch your mind.

   You might have doubts about the effectiveness of this exercise but, believe me, this is an effective one. Doing something new – like learning a craft, creating artwork, or writing short stories or poems – can help you stretch your mind. It helps you loosen up and it brings out your creativity.

Doing the abovementioned exercises on a daily basis will allow you to slowly open your third eye – but this is only the beginning. If and when you intend to master the use of your sixth sense, you have to be consistent in practicing it. Developing your third eye and further enhancing it has to form part of your lifestyle and be included in your daily routine.

The following pointers can further help you in awakening your third eye:

1. Intuition is the main purpose of your third eye, and that's why it is important to practice, exercise, and master it.

2. Reflect and meditate often in order to become better at noticing the signs your third eye is trying to show you.

3. The voice of your third eye is a whisper and this is the main reason why you have to learn how to spend time in silence and calmness. Silence and calmness can both

help you listen more attentively and successfully to what your third eye wants to convey.

4. Learn how to strengthen the energy of your throat chakra as it can help you powerfully unravel your third eye's energy.

5. As mentioned earlier, do activities that will tap into your creativity and allow your imagination to soar high.

6. Develop your mindfulness by engaging in Mindfulness Meditation Exercises. Interestingly, there are a lot of instructional videos available on the Internet regarding this subject. However, if it will be your first time to engage in such an activity, I highly suggest that you take some yoga sessions first. That way, you are guided by a professional when first doing yoga and meditation exercises. As soon as you feel comfortable doing these on your own, you can then use instructional videos as your guide. Please ensure that you do this exercise on a daily basis. Once a day for approximately thirty minutes to an hour is enough, but if you can do it more than once a day, then feel free to do so.

   Mindfulness meditation allows you to learn mindful breathing. Mindful breathing then allows you to achieve a calm mind that will eventually allow you to open your third eye. Mindful breathing also allows you to balance your chakra system.

7. Surround yourself with people who make use of their third eye as if it is a normal thing – because you will truly learn a lot from them. You will most likely find them in wellness and healing centers. There are also a number of aura readers and Reiki practitioners that can be found on the Internet in forums of Facebook groups.

8. Change or enhance the space in your home or anywhere you intend to regularly conduct your meditation. You may want to incorporate indigo – or a touch of blue and violet – in the room because indigo is the color

associated with the third eye. This may include a combination of blue and violet candles, incense, curtains, carpets, cushions, or pillows. Adding blue and/or violet lighting will definitely help set the tone. Also, you might want to start wearing clothes or accessories with a touch of indigo – such as violet or blue jewelry.

9. Create your own dream journal. It's quite difficult to remember our dreams. But if and when you are mindful about it and you practice recalling dreams on a daily basis, you will be able to remember them better. Aim to keep a dream journal by your bedside table all the time. Before you sleep every night, remind yourself that you will not forget your dreams. As soon as you wake up, recall your dream and immediately write it in your dream journal. Save enough space per journal entry so that you can later write down the interpretation of your dreams.

10. Adding fragrances that can help balance and open the chakra system is also recommended, such as the fragrances of essential oils in your home, in your bath, on your body, and in the space where you intend to hold your meditation sessions on a regular basis. Among the recommended scents are sandalwood, myrrh, Roman chamomile, grapefruit, and nutmeg.

11. Eat foods and drink beverages that come from fruits and vegetables that are violet and/or blue in color. This includes black currants, blackberries, blueberries, grapes, eggplants, prunes, rainbow chard, and beets.

Behaviors to Let Go of

Of course, if there are exercises that will help you get closer to awakening your third eye, there are also habits and behaviors that you need to give up. These include:

1. Easily giving up.

    As mentioned earlier, you need to have a lot of patience if you intend to master awakening your third eye. It is not something that will happen overnight. It takes a lot of practice, concentration, and information to be able to master it.

    Knowing how to meditate takes you a step closer to opening your third eye. However, this does not necessarily mean that you have mastered it. It's also a good idea to learn as much as you can about the different skills that can be developed through accessing your third eye. Books and videos are two of the most available tools that will augment your knowledge about the third eye, the seven chakras, Reiki, auras, dream interpretation, and astral projections, among others.

    Therefore, if you are a beginner, you have to anticipate that you have a long journey of education and practice ahead.

2. Refusing to break old habits that attract negative energies.

    Sometimes, no matter how many books a person reads about the third eye and no matter how many times he or she has attended meditation sessions, it seems as if their third eye could not be awakened. As stated in item #1, if you ever personally experience such a dilemma, you have to remember to be patient at all times. However, aside from being patient, there is also a need to help yourself in order to figure out why the strategies you have been applying don't seem to be working at all. Perhaps, one of the reasons is your failure to let go of habits that result in negative energies. These habits may include a toxic relationship; an unhealthy diet; a detrimental environment both at home and at work; and negative emotions resulting from occurrences in the past. If you are determined to develop your psychic abilities, you should learn to let go of these negative habits.

3. Absorbing negative energies.

In most cases, the people who possess negative energies are the empathic ones. They love listening to other people's concerns, they love giving pieces of advice, and more than anything else, they love putting themselves in the shoes of the problematic people they are talking to. The burdens of others become their burdens too. In other words, they easily pick up the negative energies possessed by others. If you are an empathic person, you better do something with regard to controlling your thoughts and emotions.

There is nothing wrong about expressing your concern towards others and letting them know that they are not alone in this world – it is in fact a good trait. However, if you can easily pick up the negative energies of a person, you must also learn how to easily let go of those negative energies and fill yourself with positive energies instead.

One way of making this happen is by participating in physical activity – either at the gym, through playing sport, or just jogging around the block.

Have you noticed how energetic children are and how they are filled with so much positivity? One reason for this is because they are always physically active. They're constantly playing, moving, running, hopping, jumping, and so on. You can be like them too by finding time each day to exercise. You don't necessarily have to go to the gym to do it. You can simply jog around your neighborhood or you can do exercises at home. The important thing is that you make a conscious effort to be physical on a regular basis.

4. Using meditation in a harmful way.

There are people who use meditation as a strategy to escape life. However, this is not how meditation is supposed to work especially if your aim is to hone your psychic abilities.

Meditation should help you become mindful. It is not supposed to make you escape life but, instead, it should make you live a better life.

If your aim for using meditation is to forget about the real world, this may happen if you're not careful. You must remember that meditation doesn't bring you to another world. Instead, meditation helps you open your third eye so you can see the real world in its entirety.

Chapter 3: The Art of Balancing Chakras

Chakras are the focal points in the astral body used in different ancient meditation practices. These ancient practices include Tantra, Japanese Esoteric Buddhism, Tibetan Buddhism, Chinese Taoism, and Indian religion. These practices have been adapted in the postmodern era and are known by various names including New Age medicine, alternative medicine, and pseudomedicine, among others.

In this chapter, we will briefly discuss to you the different chakras, the impact that each chakra has on your life, and the methods for balancing them. Why is this important to discuss? It's important because as you will soon learn, your third eye is one of these chakra energy points.

WHAT ARE THE DIFFERENT TYPES CHAKRAS?

1. The Crown Chakra

This focal point is also known as Sahasrara. It is considered to be the first chakra in our astral body and is known as the "crown" because it is positioned on top of our head.

If it seems that you can't find the meaning of life anymore, this means that your Crown Chakra is unbalanced. If, on the contrary, you appreciate the beauty of life and you can clearly identify your purpose in life, this means that you have a balanced Crown Chakra.

The Crown Chakra is associated with the violet lotus.

2. The Third Eye

The third eye, as mentioned earlier, is one of our chakras. It is known as the third eye as it is positioned near the eyes, just between the eyebrows.

If you worry about your future excessively and you have an unreasonable fear of ghosts or spirits, there are most likely blockages in your third eye. These blockages can also prevent you from facing the truth. There are, however, methods to address this problem that also help to hone your intuitive faculties.

The third eye is associated with the indigo lotus.

3. The Throat Chakra

This focal point is positioned at your throat's base and is linked to your communication and creative skills. If it seems as if you are having difficulty expressing your emotions and listening to others, it is because there are blockages in this chakra.

The throat chakra is associated with the blue lotus.

4. The Heart Chakra

This focal point is apparently positioned at the heart and is linked to your ability to express love and compassion. The blockages found in this chakra oftentimes – if not most of the time – result from experiences of trauma, betrayal, and breakups. A healthy heart chakra, on the contrary, allows you to experience self-acceptance, self-love, and unconditional love.

The heart chakra is associated with the green lotus.

5. *The Solar Plexus*

The Solar Plexus Chakra is positioned in the abdominal region in the middle of the rib cage. It is linked to your personal strength and power. It is also linked to your digestive system. Blockages in this chakra will physically weaken you. It is associated to several health problems including, but not limited to, diabetes, ulcers, and other forms of stomach aches.

The solar plexus is associated with the yellow lotus.

6. *The Sacral Chakra*

This focal point is positioned near the genitals as well as the navel. It is associated with health issues that affect urinary function, the reproductive system, and sexuality, among others. Like the throat chakra, the sacral chakra is also connected to your creative skills. But aside from that, this focal point also has something to do with your sensual awareness. Experiences of sexual abuse may lead to blockages in this focal point.

The sacral chakra is associated with the orange lotus.

7. *The Root Chakra*

This focal point is positioned near the spine. It is considered to be the representation of the entire chakra system and, therefore, it relates to your ability to survive life in general. It focuses on your fundamental necessities such as food and shelter. An unhealthy root chakra may cause illnesses related to the spine. It may also result in insecurities as well as a fear of loss.

The root chakra is associated with the red lotus.

BALANCING CHAKRAS

Now, you are well aware that the third eye is only one of the seven different chakras. While this book may focus on awakening your third eye, it is important to know that all chakras are connected to each other. Therefore, they all have to be balanced in order for you to open and use your third eye successfully.

There are several methods to balance chakras. Some of the common ones are meditation, yoga, breathing exercises such as pranayama, and holistic or alternative medicine. There are also healing methods that can be used, such as Reiki Healing, Craniosacral Therapy, and Pranic Healing.

Balancing your chakras is important to your daily life as it helps you improve or maintain a positive energy level. Every single day, you are exposed to different activities which can make you stressed out by the end of the day. No matter how much energy you have in the morning and no matter how interesting your activities may be, you might feel tired by the end of the day causing your energy level to go down. More often than not, no matter how productive you may be at the end of the day, there will always be stumbling blocks along the way that lower your energy. Such low energy levels, if not addressed immediately, can pile up each day and compound. Slowly, you can find yourself creeping towards a low point in life. That's why you have to learn how to balance your chakras before it's too late. Additionally, a balanced chakra system means that you are physically, mentally, and spiritually stable.

Create an environment conducive for meditation

If you are truly serious about balancing your chakras and meditating on a daily basis, I suggest that you create a space at your home that is specifically meant for meditation.

Of course, it's a good idea to first enroll in meditation or yoga sessions to learn how to do the exercises properly. That's a great way to get started, but once you feel comfortable with yoga and meditation, it's much more convenient to perform these activities at home.

You should aim to create a space that promotes calmness and relaxation. Incorporate lighting effects featuring colors that remind you of the chakra system. For instance, you may choose to incorporate an emerald green lighting as the color is associated to the restoration of your physical body.

You may incorporate a violet lighting effect too as the color will remind you to detach yourself from painful experiences. Violet is said to be a combination of three colors: sapphire blue that represents the Divine Masculine, rose pink that represents the Divine Feminine, and gold that represents Christ Consciousness.

A pink rose lighting effect would also be great in your meditation space, especially if you are longing for inner healing or inner child protection. Pink rose is associated to your relationship with the Divine Mother.

A yellow lighting that reminds you of sunshine is recommended too. It is associated with Divine Illumination and Divine Wisdom.

A gold lighting effect is also recommended as it promotes peace in its truest sense. Gold is a color that can stabilize all energy fields.

It is up to you if you want to include all or only some of the abovementioned colors. The important thing is that your lighting effectively brings inner peace and calmness.

Aside from lights, the abovementioned colors can also be used for the other items that you will display in your meditation area. For instance, you may decide to hang violet and pink rose curtains. You may place a large emerald green carpet if you like and fill the area with scented yellow and gold candles and incense. Of course, you may add coffee tables, couches, or cushions. It's all up to you. Again, the important thing here is that the area successfully promotes peace and calmness.

I also suggest that you play soft and relaxing music. Instrumental music is highly recommended.

Mindfulness Meditation

Mindfulness meditation is one type of meditation that enables you to be fully aware of what happens around you and what happens to you up to the smallest detail. First, it enables you to be conscious of everything that you do including the way you breathe, the way you are seated, and all the other things that you have never noticed before. Then, it enables you to be conscious of how the objects around you are positioned. For instance, can you specifically describe now how your night lamp is positioned on top of your bedside table? Probably not. Well, with mindfulness meditation, you will learn to be fully conscious of everything – and this will enable you to awaken your third eye.

Now, let me discuss to you two types of mindfulness meditation.

1. Body and Sound Meditation

Begin by finding your most comfortable position – this could be by sitting, standing, or lying down. Then, slightly look down. You don't have to close your eyes and bow your head. You simply have to lower your eyes without moving your head. If you are sitting or standing up, you may simply look at the floor. Remember that you must be at your most comfortable state. Do not move your gaze.

Now, be mindful of how each of your body part is positioned. Is your neck slightly bent to the right or to the left? If it is indeed bent, slowly straighten its position.

Is your right shoulder higher than your left shoulder? If it is, gently fix your stance in such a way that your shoulders are evenly positioned.

Are you slouching? If you are, sit up straight or stand up straight. If you are lying down, straighten your position.

Where are your hands placed? If you are sitting down, are your hands on your lap? How is each finger positioned? You don't have to look at your hands. Just feel. Your eyes should be focused where they have been from the very start.

How are your legs positioned? How about your feet and your toes?

Then, be mindful of the way you breathe. Be aware of how you breathe in air and how you breathe it out. Be mindful of how your heart beats. Is it beating fast or slow? Breathe deeply and slowly to calm your heartbeat.

Now, listen to the different sounds around you. Is there silence? Are there birds chirping? Can you hear leaves rustling outside the window? Are you playing soft music? Can you hear yourself breathe?

Be mindful of all of these things. If you suddenly notice that you lose your focus, just bring yourself back to focusing on your breath. During your first few tries, you will find yourself losing focus several times. Don't lose patience. It happens to everyone. Even experienced meditators lose focus at times. Whenever your mind starts wandering, bring yourself back to focusing on your breath, and go from there.

Do these exercises for approximately five to ten minutes on a daily basis. However, if you feel like doing it more than once a day, or for a longer duration, feel free to do so. The main thing is that you consistently meditate each and every day. You can do these exercises as often as you want.

2. Loving Meditation

Start this exercise by finding your most comfortable seating position. The objective of this exercise is to allow you to cultivate positive emotions.

This is a simple exercise as you are only required to think of something or someone that makes you feel genuinely happy. For instance, you start thinking of a certain song that never fails to make you happy every time you hear it. You may also think of a person who always makes you smile and laugh. Many people choose to think of their young children or pets, because they love you unconditionally and are rarely associated with negative emotions.

Imagine as if the thing, pet, or person is right in front of you. Be mindful of their features. How are they positioned right in front of you? Be mindful of the physical appearance of the person in your mind. How big or small are their eyes? How long is their hair? What are they wearing?

Then, be mindful of how you feel every time you think of that certain song, object, person, or pet. Do you feel the warmth? Do you feel happy? Do they make you smile? Do you love what you feel? Be mindful of how your heart beats. Be thankful for feeling good.

Now, say something. If you choose an object, place, or song, say something about that object or song. If you choose a person or a pet, say something directly to them. Talk to them. Make a wish for them – for example, wish for them to have good health, to be safe always, to be happy always, and so on. Find good things to say to them and about them. Observe how this exercise makes you feel good.

Then, focus your mental image on yourself. Talk to yourself. Wish yourself well – to have good health, to be safe always, to be happy always, and so on. Find good things to say to yourself and about yourself. Observe how this exercise also makes you feel good.

Now, ask yourself what else could make you happier in your life. Will it make you happier if your family members develop a closer relationship? Will it make you happier if you have a better job? Will it make you happier if you know that your friends and family have better lives?

With your current mental image, talk to them and wish them all well. Wish them to be filled with joy and love at all times. Wish them to have freedom from sorrows and fear. Wish them success. If your mental image includes your wish to have a better job, talk to yourself once again and wish yourself to have a better professional life. The main point of this exercise is to promote love and kindness.

Do this exercise for at least ten minutes. However, if you can do it for more than ten minutes, please do so.

Some meditation practitioners and students do this exercise with their eyes closed. If you prefer to have your eyes open, that's okay too. Whatever helps you to focus is the best.

You can do this exercise often throughout your day. For example, while you're on your way to work you could use the time to think of happy thoughts and wish well for others. Some people even do this exercise during their lunch break, while walking on the sidewalk on their way to the restaurant or cafeteria. Every time they find some free time, they try to squeeze in doing this exercise. That way, they maintain a positive aura throughout the day, and transmit good vibes to other people.

I highly suggest that you strictly do these two types of mindfulness meditation for three to four weeks before trying any other forms of meditation. This will help you develop the habit of daily meditation and prepare you for further unlocking your third eye and developing your psychic abilities.

Chakra Meditation

This type of meditation will allow you to balance your entire chakra system. Remember, stick to the mindfulness meditation for a few weeks before moving on to this more advanced meditation practice.

Here are the step-by-step instructions to do this chakra meditation:

1. Find a place conducive for meditation. If you have a meditation area at home, use it. Otherwise, find an alternative quiet place where you can hold your chakra meditation.

2. You have to find a comfortable seating position. You may opt to sit up straight in a chair or to sit on the floor with your legs crossed.

3. Gently close your eyes, be mindful of the way you breathe, and relax your body and mind.

4. As you breathe in and breathe out, be mindful of the way you are sitting down. Be mindful of how much weight you put on the chair or on the floor.

5. Similar to how you do the mindfulness meditation exercises, be mindful of each of your body part. Be

mindful of the sounds around you. Be mindful of your lighting. Be mindful of the air circulating inside the room.

6. Create a mental image of the sky above you and of the surroundings just right outside your home or right where you are doing your chakra meditation.

7. Relax your mind. Let your mind release negative thoughts and images. Let your body release all emotions and feelings. Clear your mind and body. Just simply be mindful of the things that this exercise instructs you to do.

8. Be mindful of how your body weight rests just below your spine and into the root chakra. Create a mental image with red as the dominant color.

9. Move your mental image up towards your stomach and gradually focus on your sacral chakra. Incorporate the orange color in your mental image. This promotes motivation, empowerment, and balance.

10. Gradually move your mental image up toward your rib cage and focus on your solar plexus. Imagine yourself bathing under the sun as this is the most ideal way of incorporating the yellow color in your mental image. This promotes replenishment, restoration, and nourishment. With your current mental image, remind yourself that you greatly value yourself.

11. Repeat the same process but this time move on to your heart chakra. Tell yourself that you will freely give love to everyone and that you will always feel completely loved. Imagine yourself expressing love to everyone as others reciprocate what you express to them. Incorporate the green color in your mental image as you highlight nourishment, renewal, and healing.

12. Move on to your throat chakra. Dominate your mental image with the shade of blue. Remember that the throat chakra promotes personal will and self-expression. You

may imagine yourself sitting by the beach under the deep blue skies. Tell yourself that you will always hear and speak the truth. Remind yourself to always genuinely express yourself.

13. Now, move on to your sixth sense – or your third eye. Tell yourself that things shall unravel as they should. Remind yourself to see good things that are beyond what the naked eye can see. Fill your mental image with the shade of indigo. This chakra highlights wisdom and intuition.

14. Finally, you have reached the top chakra – commonly known as the crown chakra. Shift the shade of your mental image from indigo to violet. Confidently tell yourself that you are one with the universe. Tell yourself that you are a perfect being and that you are whole and complete.

15. Once again, be mindful of the sounds around you. Be mindful of your posture. Observe how positive your aura has become. Now, gently open your eyes.

Earlier, you were advised to practice mindfulness meditation at least once a day, every day. But if you can practice it more than once in a day, I highly encourage that too. However, when it comes to the chakra meditation, I don't suggest that you practice this every day. This should only be done if and when you feel as if you need to clean, balance, and restore your chakras. Many practitioners choose to do this once a month.

Chapter 4: Getting Acquainted with Your Higher Self

In this chapter, you will learn about your Higher Self and how you can become acquainted with it.

Your Higher Self is actually your own spirit which possesses the gifts of clairvoyance, intuition, and the like. In order to master the use of your Higher Self, you need the help of your subconscious.

Did you know that your subconscious is more powerful than your conscious mind? And I mean, *way more* powerful. Your subconscious mind has the ability to store all your past experiences – both good and bad. If you want to awaken your Higher Self, you must quiet your lower self which is your ego. In doing so, you have to let go of the negative emotions inside you that were brought about by your negative past experiences.

When I say you must quiet your ego, it means that you should learn to let go. Learn to forget, to forgive, and to trust. Learn to stop ranting, whining, judging, and blaming others and yourself. In other words, learn to move on and learn to focus more on the beauty of life.

Here are some initial steps on how to let go of ego, and become in touch with your Higher Self:

1. Express your strong belief that there is indeed a Higher Self that you can communicate with. You have to have a conviction and positivity that talking to your Higher Self on a daily basis will greatly improve the relationship of your physical body with your spirit. This will eventually lead you to improve your inner growth.

2. Improve the way you view the world. We are all aware that we are living in a materialistic world. There is always a price to pay in order to survive in the real world. Sadly, this prevents us from realizing that there is also a spiritual realm that needs our attention too. Learn all you can about spirituality and the spiritual realm.

3. Embrace solitude. Find joy and relaxation in being alone. This is one of the reasons why you should create a meditation area at home. This way, you can practice being alone in one area and enjoying every bit of the experience.

   Practice this activity by simply sitting alone at your meditation area or anywhere else conducive for meditation. Do nothing and expect nothing. Just sit in silence. Free your mind from problems and from all your To-Do's.

   Listen to your inner voice as it always has something to say to you. It will give you important details that you need. It will provide insight that will ultimately help you in making decisions. It will allow things to happen – things that are in your favor. Many, if not all, of the successful people in the world have been known for taking the time to be alone in solitude. They have always been known to consistently find the time to improve their relationship with their inner self.

4. Do meditation exercises on a daily basis. We have discussed this in the previous chapter. However, there are many forms of meditation exercises to choose from. You might want to familiarize yourself with a few of those and choose the ones that suit you best. As mentioned earlier, the best way to learn about the different meditation techniques is by first attending meditation and yoga classes conducted by professional

instructors. You will definitely learn a lot from them – not only the different meditation and yoga postures, but also about the interior design of their meditation room, the scent they use that promotes calmness, and the background music that they play.

5. Keep a journal. Write down not only about how you feel on a daily basis, but right down also your insights and your goals. Most importantly, always document your dreams on a daily basis. At first, this might seem difficult to do because, in most cases, we tend to forget about our dreams as soon as we wake up. One piece of advice is to say this aloud before you sleep, "I promise to remember my dreams as soon as I wake up." During the first few days, you might still fail to remember your dreams. Don't lose hope. Just consistently tell yourself to remember your dreams and in the morning, always try your best to remember your dreams. Then, write them down right away in your journal – that's why it is best to keep your journal by your bedside table. Updating your journal should form part of your morning and evening rituals.

    You have to document your dreams because dreams have interpretations. Your dreams might be telling you something that you just keep on ignoring. It is also best that in your journal, you leave enough space after each journal entry so that you can go back to your previous entries to jot down the interpretations of your dreams.

    Make it a habit to not only document the things that transpire each day. Document your goals and your action plans too. Write all your thoughts. That way, your mind and body are always aligned to your goals.

6. Constantly communicate with your Higher Self. At first, you might feel as if you are fooling yourself and that it

seems like a one-way communication. Continue talking to your inner self even if you don't get any reply. Eventually, you will be amazed at how the answers to your questions present themselves. Be mindful in listening to your inner voice. Sooner or later, you will learn to unravel your Higher Self.

7. Learn from life lessons. Live life each day with the mentality that you were born to experience the goodness of life. If something bad occurs, always exert your effort to discover the lessons behind your bad experiences. If and when good things happen to you, never fail to discover the lessons from those too.

Chapter 5: Trusting Your Instincts

Instinct or intuition refers to your ability to gain knowledge even without conscious reasoning or evidence. In fact, how you acquire that knowledge is also beyond your understanding.

It seems as if there is a tiny voice that you hear over and over again inside your head. It seems that there is a tingling sensation under your skin. It seems as if your mind and body are telling you something. If and when you experience these things, do not just ignore them. Listen to that tiny voice and understand what you feel. However, you must be able to interpret it correctly. The key to doing this is to be mindful of everything that happens to you, everything that happens in you, and everything that happens around you. This is the reason why mindfulness meditation is significant to your decision to hone the use of your third eye as well as your psychic abilities.

Here are some pointers about paying attention to your gut feelings:

1. **Be mindful about how your body feels.**

    Do you feel good or do you feel as if something's wrong?

    Do you ever experience moments when it seems as if you feel weak or that something is toxic, but you just can't seem to clearly identify what you exactly feel? But just because you can't pinpoint exactly what is wrong, this doesn't mean that you should simply ignore what you feel. The worst thing that might happen is for a small issue to become a big dilemma all because of negligence.

    Be aware that physical symptoms have meanings.

    For instance, never ignore it if you feel like your energy level is declining every time you are near a specific person. Have you ever spent time with a person who makes you sleepy despite them being a jolly person? Have you also spent time with a person who brings you joy in spite of them being a "man of few words"? You see, just because a person looks jolly, it doesn't necessarily mean that he or she exudes a positive aura. In the same way that just because a person is quiet or seems boring, it doesn't necessarily mean that he or she exudes a negative aura.

This is what the adage "Looks can be deceiving" means in its truest sense. Therefore, it is only right to be mindful and vigilant of everything at all times. Focus on what you feel, and not just what you see.

2. **Do not ignore the feeling of danger.**

Do you ever experience feeling uneasy every time you are near a particular person?

Do you ever experience feeling uneasy about someone you just met?

Do you ever experience feeling uneasy standing or sitting beside a stranger? This doesn't happen with every stranger. But every so often there will be someone that makes you feel uncomfortable as if something bad is going to happen.

During times like this, you have to listen to your intuition, and act before something bad does happen.

3. **Do not ignore the feeling of danger even if it is not about you.**

You should learn to detect danger not only if it involves you but also if it involves other people. There is a part of your brain that allows you to think about the feelings of other people, and experience empathy. If you learn to interpret these feelings the right way, you will learn to sense whether or not someone needs your help badly. Your gut feeling will also be able to guide you on what kind of help you should extend to those in danger.

Being able to help others has a positive impact on you. It helps you become happier, and it remarkably improves your well-being.

4. **Do not neglect your positive gut feeling.**

We have been talking a lot about being mindful to prevent bad things from happening. Well, we should also put emphasis on being mindful to allow good things to happen.

If you feel genuinely positive about people and the opportunities they present, then you should take these opportunities! Spend time with those that exude positive energy, and in turn they will help your energy to become more positive and vibrant!

Chapter 6: Learning about Personal Meditation

In this chapter, we will focus on the different types of meditation that will allow you to experience personal improvement. These meditation exercises will help you become attuned with yourself. These exercises will enable you to connect with your Higher Self. If, and when, you have a balanced chakra system and you have a perfectly attuned self, you will find it easier to trust your instinct or your intuition.

Higher-Self Meditation

This meditation exercise lasts for a minimum of thirty minutes – you, of course, have the option to do it for longer than thirty minutes. As long as you feel more and more positive about doing the exercise, feel free to do it over and over again.

Begin by finding your most comfortable position – you can be standing up, sitting down, or lying down. Make sure that you are also wearing comfortable clothes.

Now, close your eyes and focus on the way you breathe. Let your stomach expand as you take a deep breath, and let it wane as you exhale.

Keep your mind focused and relaxed. If you notice that your mind gets distracted and starts to think of something else, just focus your mind back on the way you breathe and the way your stomach expands and shrinks. From time to time, you will notice your mind deviating to other mental images. If this happens, just bring your attention back to your breath.

Now, create a mental image of yourself under a big tree. Make the tree so large that its branches exaggeratedly extend up to the sky – as if the tree is trying to connect you to your Higher Self.

Now, imagine a beautiful angel appearing right in front of you under the tree. Imagine it to be your Higher Self. It is beautifully glowing and genuinely smiling at you. Ask it to combine with you.

Then, imagine it transforming into a golden ball that moves directly at you and inside you. It enters your body through your crown chakra. Feel the warm energy entering and covering your entire body. Your Higher Self is now one with you.

Try to ask questions to your Higher Self and observe how it responds to you. Its response will most likely be through images, words, or feelings. You have to be mindful and attentive to prevent yourself from missing the hints it gives you. The answers might take time to unravel right before you, but one thing is for sure; your Higher Self will always communicate with you.

At first, you might feel weird about doing this but, sooner or later, you will get the hang of it and start to notice that your connection with your Higher Self becomes stronger and stronger.

End the exercise by wiggling your fingers and toes. Be mindful of how you wiggle them. Be mindful of how you breathe in and breathe out. Then, gently open your eyes.

Do this exercise every day as it will help you clear your mind. This exercise is also ideal if and when you feel that you need guidance in life.

Laughter Meditation

This meditation exercise lasts for a minimum of twelve minutes. It is composed of three parts in which the first part is stretching, the second part is laughing, and the last part is stillness.

It is advisable that you do this exercise first thing in the morning right before you eat breakfast. However, if this is not feasible, make sure you do this before you eat your lunch or dinner.

1. Stretching

Stretch your body as much as you can. Stand on your toes. Then, clasp your hands together and, while your fingers are intertwined, stretch your arms right above your head and allow your palms to face upward. Hold this position for ten seconds, and then release.

Slowly and repeatedly close and open your mouth to stretch the muscles of your face and your jaw. The best way to do this is by yawning.

2. Laughing

After that jaw exercise, slowly turn up the corners of your mouth to form a small smile. Then, make a bigger smile – first, without showing your teeth, then, eventually showing them. Then, start laughing but not forcefully.

At first, you might feel weird laughing without any reason but, after a while, you will realize that it is indeed therapeutic to laugh.

It is alright to do this exercise with a partner. In fact, it is more fun to do this with someone. But you have to keep in mind that you are supposed to laugh for no reason at all. If you are with a partner, don't laugh at each other but, instead, laugh with each other. Do not laugh about anyone or anything. Just laugh for the sake of this exercise. Be mindful of how you laugh. Be mindful of how laughter makes you feel inside. Be mindful of how laughter makes you feel good. Laugh for at least five minutes.

3. Stillness

After five minutes, cease from laughing and slowly close your eyes. Do not make unnecessary movements. Be as still as possible.

Then, find a comfortable position. You may continue standing if you want. You may choose to sit down or lie down. In this type of exercise, most people find lying down is best.

Observe the silence and feel the good sensation that the silence brings you. Observe how it relaxes you. If you notice your mind deviating to other things, bring back your attention to the exercise. Just clear your mind and appreciate the silence and the clarity of the mind and body that it gives you.

Sleep Meditation

1. This exercise begins by lying down in bed, on the floor, or on a yoga mat with your eyes closed.

2. Just like any other mindfulness meditation, you are instructed to be mindful of how you are positioned. Be mindful of how you breathe. Breathe through your nose as you inhale and breathe out using your mouth. Be mindful of the sensations that you feel while lying down. Do you feel a tingling sensation? Is the room temperature hot or cold? Do you feel any pressure? Can you feel how your stomach expands and shrinks as you inhale and exhale? Is a body part itchy?

3. Now, pay attention more to each part of your body. Begin with your fingers, specifically with your right thumb. Do you feel any sensation? Is it itchy? How is it positioned? Notice as many details as you can. Then, move on to your index finger and do the same process.

Then, move on through the next fingers until you complete your right hand.

4. Shift your attention to your right wrist, and then move on to your right arm, to your right shoulder, and then the entire right part of your body until you reach your right foot and toes. Once done, do the same process to your left body parts, beginning with the left thumb.

5. Do not exert any effort to analyze or understand what you feel or how each body part is positioned. Merely notice and observe them.

6. Don't forget to always be mindful of the way you breathe too. Observe how relaxed you feel. If in case you notice that a body part seems tense, breathe deeply until your body relaxes.

7. Don't forget to be mindful of all the parts of your head, beginning with the chin all the way up to the crown.

8. Notice how this exercise makes you feel relaxed. Savor the moment. Continue to lie down and relax.

9. Then, repeat the process all over again. Be mindful again of each part of your body beginning with your right thumb once again.

10. Repeat the process at least twice, though there is no limit as to how many times you can repeat this meditation.

Chapter 7: The Myths about Psychic Powers

Psychic phenomena, as we all know, cannot be clearly explained by the laws of science. While scientists cannot find adequate evidence to prove the existence of such phenomena, there are nonetheless occurrences that cannot be explained by science alone and, thus, fall under the category of pseudoscience. However, due to the fact that more and more people are reporting having these experiences, scientists have begun exploring this subject.

Many people may not believe in psychic phenomena, but numerous people nonetheless do. Believe it or not, many of them are the rich and famous people that we know of such as actresses Angelina Jolie, Cameron Diaz, and Sarah Jessica Parker. Of course, there are also famous businesspeople such as Henry Ford and Bill Gates. All of them believe that such phenomena have had a big impact on their exceptional success.

In this day and age, many people have started to develop and practice their psychic skills. They positively believe that it guides them in making decisions. They strongly believe that through their psychic abilities, they prevent big problems from occurring and they enable themselves to always choose the right path.

In spite of the popularity of psychic phenomena, there are still of course people who strongly oppose it – thus, the existence of myths about psychic skills.

In this chapter we will dispel a few of the common myths about psychic abilities:

1. People with psychic skills are evil.

Having psychic skills is a natural ability that any human being can possess. Just like any other skill, psychic skills can also be developed and can form part of your daily life.

In order to develop your psychic skills, you have to bring out all the positive energy inside you. That's why before you possess this skill, you have to meditate and let go of all the negativities whether they are spiritual, mental, or physical. Otherwise, you will not be able to develop this skill. This only means that possessing psychic skills means that you are a positive person.

Evil, on the contrary, is all about negativity. Therefore, you cannot be evil if you possess psychic skills. Clearly, this is a myth.

2. Not everyone can possess psychic skills.

To reiterate, having psychic skills is a natural ability that any human being can possess. If you are determined and strongly driven to awaken your third eye and develop your psychic abilities, you will doubtlessly possess this skill. It's just like any other goals in life that you have. If you are totally driven to reach your goal, you will do everything to achieve it.

Perhaps, there is some truth to this myth. While we are all capable of developing this skill, we have different levels of determination. Again, this is pretty much like any other skill that we would like to hone. For instance, if you claim that you are interested in developing your verbal communication skill but you do not strictly follow the exercises that you need to do to help you improve, chances are that you will not succeed in developing such skill.

3. Developing psychic skills takes years.

The duration of developing your psychic skills actually depends on nobody but you. It all depends on how disciplined you are in following the exercises and all the other tasks related to develop such skill.

Sometimes, a person's mind says that they are one hundred per cent determined to hone their skill, but their actual performance shows otherwise. For example, they don't practice meditation every day but instead do it only every other day. Next, he or she might finish the 30-minute meditation exercise after just 15-minutes. This kind of behavior will not remove all negative energy. It will definitely not balance your chakras. It will not awaken your third eye and, therefore, will not allow you to hone your psychic skills.

However, if you are determined to develop your psychic skills as soon as possible and you express your determination through your dedication to performing the exercises, you will hone your skills in no time at all.

Therefore, to generalize that all beginners will take years to hone their psychic skills is a myth. Nobody can gauge your ability to learn, but you.

4. People with psychic skills are freaks.

Sometimes, psychics are stereotyped as freaks or crazy people mainly because of how they are represented in movies or in television shows. But you should realize that what you watch on TV and in movies are exaggerated portrayals of psychics.

It is not true that if you have psychic powers, you will have the ability to see zombies, ghosts, and other scary creatures you see in fantasy and horror movies and television shows.

In reality, psychics are not freaks. Therefore, this is also a myth.

Chapter 8: Developing Your Psychic Skills

In the previous chapters, you learned about several meditation exercises. In this chapter, you will learn more but, this time, the exercises will strictly help you awaken your third eye and develop your psychic abilities.

The exercises that we will discuss in this chapter all fall under the Healing Meditation Exercises. If and when you open your third eye and hone your psychic skills, you will have the ability to heal yourself and others. But, of course, you have to begin with yourself before you can help others.

If and when you find the exercises confusing, feel free to stop, rest, and relax. Remember that these exercises are meant to emit positive energies and not negative ones.

I advise that you do these meditation exercises in a quiet and comfortable place.

Meditation to Release Anger

This exercise aims to address any hatred that exists inside of you. This often can be hatred that you thought never existed but has long been there inside you unconsciously.

While sitting or lying down comfortably, gently close your eyes and be mindful of how you breathe. Start the deep breathing exercise – inhaling through your nose and exhaling through your mouth. Allow your stomach to expand as you inhale and allow it to wane as you exhale. Do this repeatedly until you feel fully relaxed.

Every time you inhale, create a mental image of a white ray of light inside the room. As you exhale, imagine that you are releasing all the hatred kept inside your body. Imagine that, as you exhale, you also release all the negativities you have inside you.

Then, create a mental image of you sitting inside a dark movie theatre. Imagine that the movie you are watching focuses on the pain and anger you felt from your childhood up to the present. All the scenarios in which you were hurt by people are being flashed on the movie screen. The faces of all the people who have hurt you are there flashing right before your very eyes.

Then, create a mental image of yourself looking around the movie theatre and noticing that you are not alone in the room. There are other people watching with you. You try to get a clear vision of each of the people around you and learn that they are in fact the people who have hurt you in the past. They are the people featured in the movie that all of you are watching. Then, you notice that they seem to get affected by what they are watching. Everyone is either crying or teary-eyed because they could feel the pain that they have caused you. You can hear them say sorry.

Then, create a mental image of you approaching the nearest person. Genuinely tell him or her that you have forgiven them, and that you are willing to forget the pain that they've caused you. Hug them. If you feel like crying, don't stop yourself from crying. Take your time. Don't be in a hurry. Continue this mental image until you have fully released the pain you feel inside.

Then, approach another person inside the movie theatre and repeat the same process. Do this repeatedly until you have approached every person who has hurt you in the past. Once you have truly forgiven all of them, imagine the lights inside the theatre turning back on.

Now, bring yourself back to consciousness by paying attention once again to your body. Move your toes and your fingers. Be mindful of how you breathe. Then, gently open your eyes.

This exercise is expected to last for a minimum of twenty minutes. But then again, please take your time. The objective of this exercise is to one hundred percent release any and all hatred inside of you.

Meditation to Release Fear and Anxiety

This exercise aims to address your feelings of fear and anxiety. This exercise also provides psychic protection. When you eventually learn how to use your psychic abilities, there are unexpected occurrences that might scare you or stress you out. That's why it is best that you address your fear and anxiety first by performing this meditation technique. This technique will remind you not to panic and to always be in control.

While sitting or lying down comfortably, gently close your eyes and be mindful of how you breathe. Start applying the deep breathing exercise – inhaling through your nose and exhaling through your mouth. Allow your stomach to expand as you inhale and allow it to wane as you exhale. Do this repeatedly until you feel fully relaxed.

As you continue your deep breathing exercise, create a mental image of a violet light coming down right from the sky and straight into your head. Imagine the light moving around inside your head, taking away all your fears and anxieties. As this happens, talk to the light and instruct it to remove your negative energies permanently.

Think of a happy thought. It could be an image of your children, or your favorite food, or even a beautiful a tourist destination. It doesn't matter what kind of image you want to create in your mind. The important thing is that it makes you happy and there is no negative thought that will enter you mind every time you think about it.

Now, bring yourself back to consciousness by paying attention once again to your body. Move your toes and your fingers. Be mindful of how you breathe. Then, gently open your eyes.

This exercise is expected to last for a minimum of fifteen minutes. But then again, please take your time. The objective of this exercise is to totally release all the fear and anxiety inside you.

Meditation to Release Tension

This exercise aims to relax both your mind and body. It aims to remove all the tension and ultimately allow you to feel relaxed.

This exercise is best done while sitting comfortably. Just like most other meditation exercises, you first need to gently close your eyes and be mindful of how you breathe. Start once again applying the deep breathing exercise – inhaling through your nose and exhaling through your mouth. Allow your stomach to expand as you inhale and allow it to wane as you exhale. Do this repeatedly until you feel fully relaxed.

Be mindful of the tingling sensation in your feet. If there is no tingling sensation, just be mindful of how relaxed your feet are. You can also create a mental image of yourself soaking your feet into a bathtub. Imagine how relaxing that feels in real life.

Now, imagine that particular relaxing feeling moving up from your feet to your ankles, then to your legs, to your knees, to your thighs, and so on and so forth. Make sure that you allow each part of your body to feel that sensation until you reach the top of your head.

Also, pay special attention to your spine. Allow your back to feel one hundred percent relaxed. Notice how your deep breathing helps you relax. Do this repeatedly until you don't feel any body tension anymore. In the event that there is a particular body part that needs more attention, please, take your time to release the tension.

Now, think of any health issues that you have whether they are minor or major ones. It could be a disease, pain, or injury. It can be absolutely anything that you want healed.

Picture your issues as dark areas inside your body being healed by a bright light of relaxation. Move such light across all parts of your body but pay extra attention on the dark areas. Imagine the light moving in circles on the dark areas until the dark color begin to lighten and lighten. Strongly create a mental image of the dark areas getting smaller and smaller as the bright light continues to move around them.

This exercise aims to strengthen your positive energy – so that no matter how serious your health issue may be, you can fight it by thinking positively at all times. Hold a strong belief that you have the ability to naturally heal yourself. Have that strong conviction that a genuinely positive mind can truly help you become a healthy person.

Now, bring yourself back to consciousness by paying attention once again to your body. Move your toes and your fingers. Be mindful of how you breathe. Then, gently open your eyes.

This exercise is expected to last for a minimum of thirty minutes. But once again, please take your time. The objective of this exercise is to totally release all the tension inside of you.

You also have the option to fall asleep instead of bringing yourself back to consciousness. In this case, notice how relaxed your mind and body feel upon waking up.

Conclusion

Thanks again for taking the time to read this book!

You should now have a good understanding of third eye awakening, and how to develop your psychic abilities!

If you enjoyed this book, please take the time to leave me a review on Amazon. I appreciate your honest feedback, and it really helps me to continue producing high quality books.